Pebble® Plus

HOW **ELECTRICITY** GETS FROM **POWER PLANTS** TO **HOMES**

by Megan Cooley Peterson

Consultant: A. David Salvia
Assistant Professor, Electrical Engineering
Penn State, University Park, Pennsylvania

CAPSTONE PRESS
a capstone imprint

Pebble Plus is published by Capstone Press,
1710 Roe Crest Drive, North Mankato, Minnesota 56003
www.mycapstone.com

Library of Congress Cataloging-in-Publication Data
Cataloging-in-publication information is on file with the Library of Congress.
ISBN 978-1-4914-8434-0 (library binding)
ISBN 978-1-4914-8438-8 (paperback)
ISBN 978-1-4914-8442-5 (eBook PDF)

Editorial Credits
Jill Kalz, editor; Juliette Peters and Katelin Plekkenpol, designers;
Morgan Walters, media researcher; Laura Manthe, production specialist

Photo Credits
Capstone Studio: Karon Dubke, 21; Shutterstock: Chones, 17, chungking, 7, Concept Photo,
20, CoolKengzz, 6, Dmitry Kalinovsky, 14, DomDew_Studio, 18, Givaga, 1, back cover,
Innershadows Photography, Cover, jakit17, 13, Karkas, 8, leisuretime70, 12, m.jrn, 10, Martin
Capek, (blue lightning) top right Cover, (transformer) top left Cover, 5, michaeljung, 15, Rido,
19, rtem, 9, Sergey Nivens, 3, Shooting Star Studio, 16, ssguy, 11, tab62, Cover, wang song,
22-23

Note to Parents and Teachers

The Here to There set supports national curriculum standards for science and social
studies related to technology and the roles of community workers. This book describes and
illustrates the journey electricity takes from power plants to homes. The images support
early readers in understanding the text. The repetition of words and phrases helps early
readers in understanding the text. This book also introduces early readers to subject-
specific vocabulary words, which are defined in the Glossary section. Early readers may
need assistance to read some words and to use the Table of Contents, Glossary, Read More,
Internet Sites, Critical Thinking Using the Common Core, and Index sections of the book.

Printed in the United States   4652

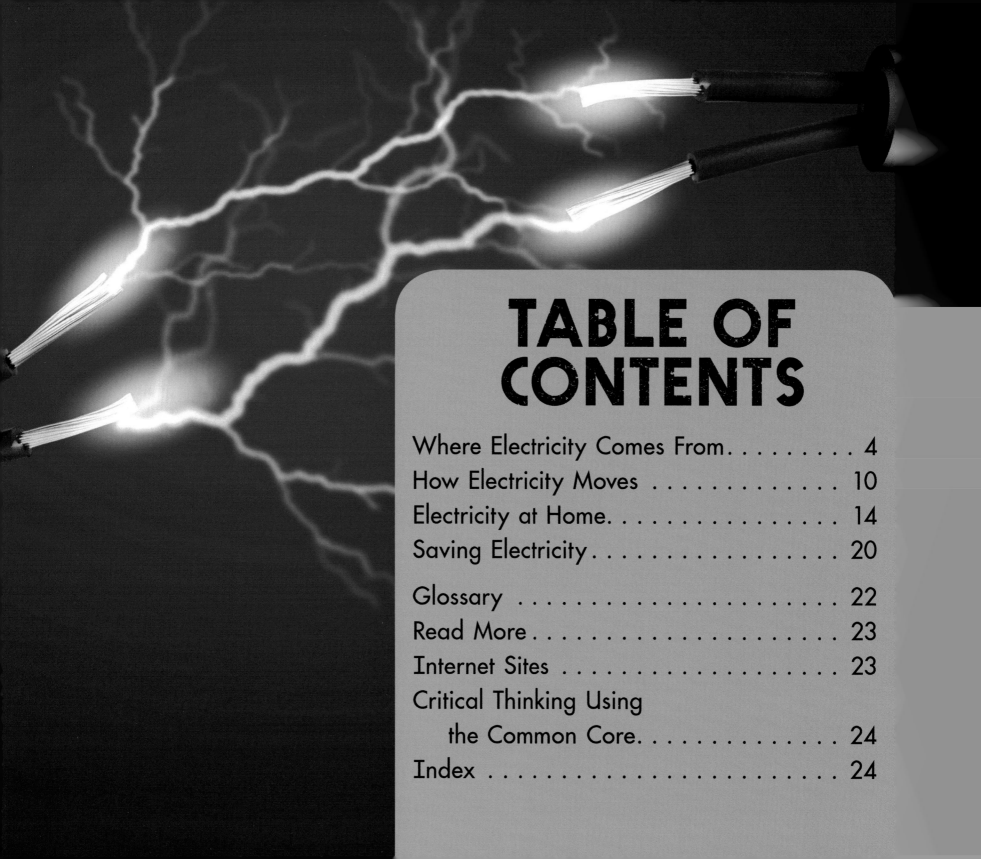

TABLE OF CONTENTS

Where Electricity Comes From

Electricity is a kind of energy that makes things work. It powers TVs, lights, and much more. Where does electricity come from?

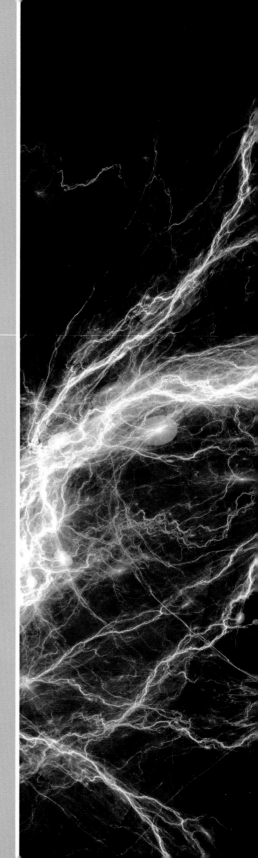

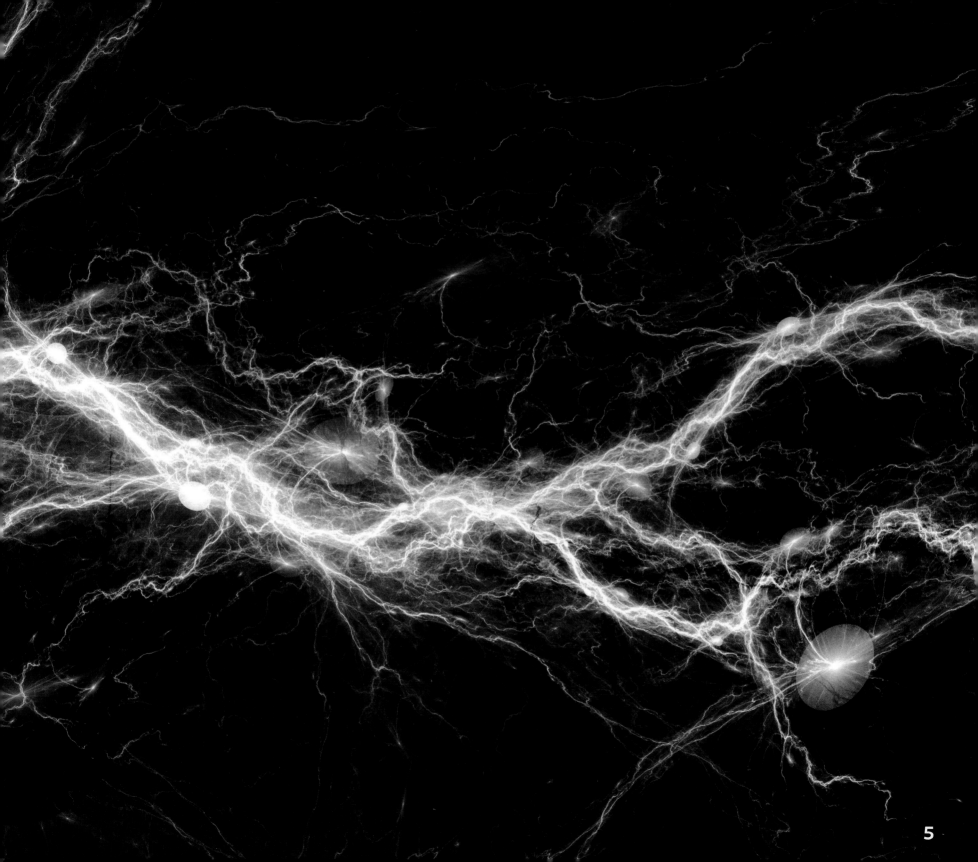

Power plants make electricity.
They make it in different ways.
One kind of power plant
boils water. The water turns
into steam.

boiler

Hiss! The steam rises quickly.

It turns a turbine. A turbine

is a large wheel with blades.

The turbine turns a generator.

The generator makes electricity.

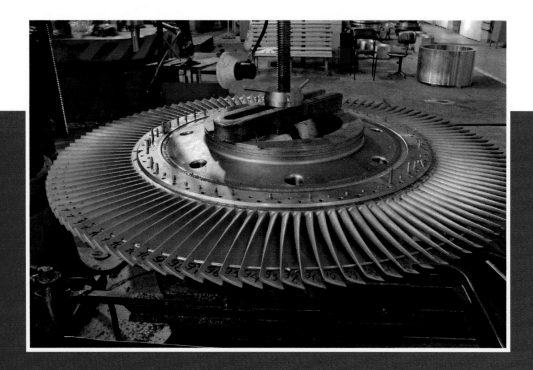

generator

How Electricity Moves

Electricity moves through

metal wires called power lines.

Some power lines hang in the air.

Other lines are buried underground.

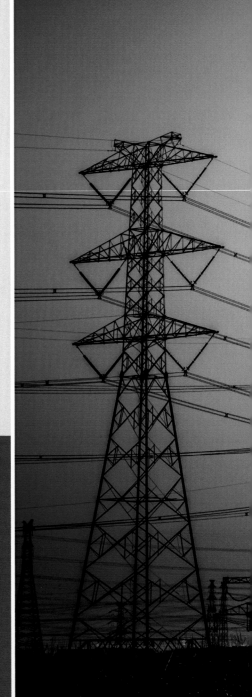

The electricity in power lines is dangerous to touch. Transformers make electricity safer to use before it enters buildings.

transformers

transformers

Electricity at Home

Electricians install wires for electricity inside buildings. They wear rubber safety shoes and gloves. The rubber keeps electricians safe from shocks.

Electricity flows through outlets in walls. When you plug in something, electricity makes it work. Flip a switch. Zing! A light bulb lights up!

A meter measures how much

electricity people use.

Meter readers check the meters.

People pay for the amount

of electricity they use.

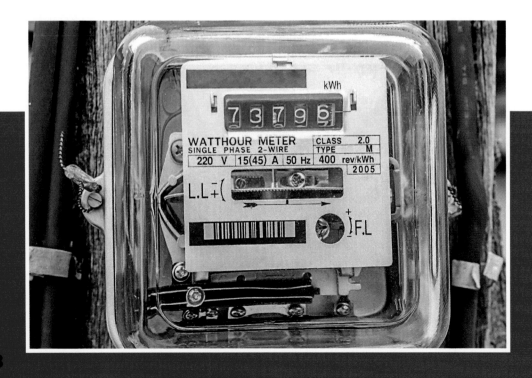

Saving Electricity

You can do your part

to save electricity. Watch less

TV. Play fewer video games.

Turn off the lights when

you leave a room.

GLOSSARY

boil—to heat water or another liquid until it bubbles; water gives off steam when it boils

electrician—someone who puts in and fixes electrical wiring in a building

electricity—a natural force that can be used to make light and heat or to make machines work

energy—the ability to do work, such as moving things or giving heat or light

generator—a machine that produces electricity by turning a magnet inside a coil of wire

install—to put in and connect for use

measure—to find out the size or strength of something

meter—a machine that keeps track of how much electricity a home or business uses

power plant—a building or group of buildings used to create electricity; some power plants burn coal or gas, while others use water, wind, or sunshine to make electricity

steam—the gas that water turns into when it boils

transformer—a device that connects power lines to buildings

turbine—an engine powered by steam, water, wind, or gas passing across the blades of a fanlike device and making it spin

READ MORE

Alpert, Barbara. *Electricity All Around.* Science Builders. Mankato, Minn.: Capstone Press, 2012.

Dawson, Patricia. *An Electrician's Job.* Community Workers. New York: Cavendish Square Publishing, 2015.

Weingarten, Ethan. *What Is a Circuit?* Electrified! New York: Gareth Stevens Pub., 2013.

INTERNET SITES

FactHound offers a safe, fun way to find Internet sites related to this book. All of the sites on FactHound have been researched by our staff.

Here's all you do:

Visit *www.facthound.com*

Type in this code: 9781491484340

Super-cool stuff!

Check out projects, games and lots more at
www.capstonekids.com

CRITICAL THINKING USING THE COMMON CORE

1. Electricity travels through power lines. Why do you think power lines hang high in the air or lie underground? (Integration of Knowledge and Ideas)

2. Explain why electricians are important. What might happen if there were no electricians? (Integration of Knowledge and Ideas)

3. Name two things you can do to save electricity. (Key Ideas and Details)

INDEX